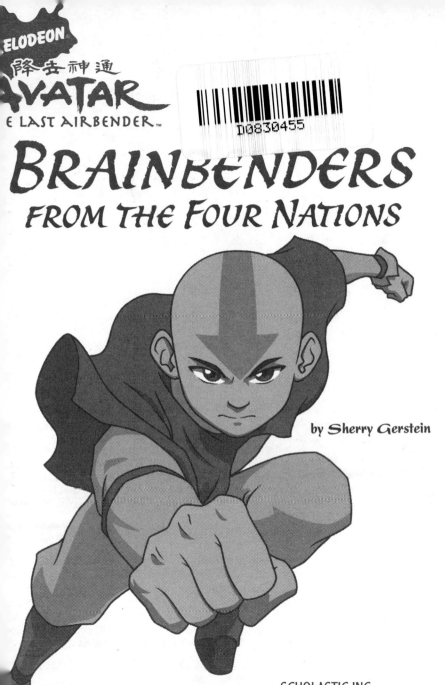

ELODEON

降去神通
VATAR
E LAST AIRBENDER™

BRAINBENDERS
FROM THE FOUR NATIONS

D0830455

by Sherry Gerstein

SCHOLASTIC INC.
New York Toronto London Auckland Sydney
Mexico City New Delhi Hong Kong Buenos Aires

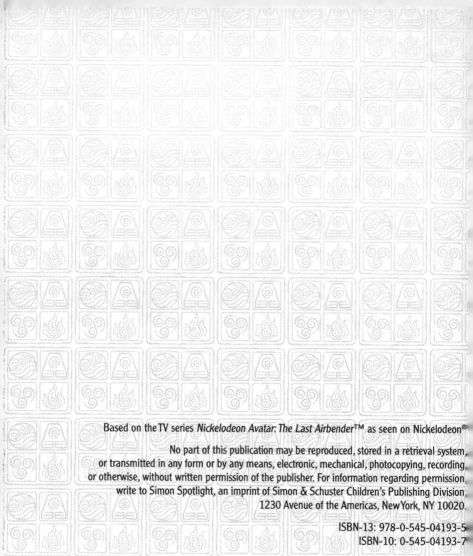

CONTENTS

TAKE THE AVATAR TRIVIA CHALLENGE!

Think you can go with the flow like a Waterbender? Or do you have a rock—solid foundation like an Earthbender? Perhaps you can blow through these quizzes like an Airbender, or blaze through them all like a Firebender. To keep score, get out a pencil and a piece of paper and jot down your answers. Then turn to the end of the book to see how well you did overall and in each category. You say you've got the skills— now put them to the test!

Season One
BOOK ONE: WATER

CAST OF CHARACTERS

Think back to the earliest episodes. Who are the main characters? What are the main events? Who said what? Here's a quick refresher course to ease you back into the Avatar world.

AANG

He's the last surviving Airbender, and the last great hope for future generations. He needs to master the four elements before he can confront the Fire Lord, but until that happens, Aang plans to make time for fun, too.

KATARA

The only Waterbender left in her village, fourteen-year-old Katara knows she must look after the children and the elderly. But she dreams of finding a teacher who can help her train to be a true Waterbending master.

SOKKA

Katara's brother may be just a regular guy with no bending abilities, but this fifteen-year-old warrior is totally ingenious when it comes to science and engineering. He's the idea guy that everyone turns to when they need solutions.

ZUKO

This seventeen-year-old son of the Fire Lord is focused on one thing only. Banished from the Fire Nation by his own father, he seeks to restore his honor by capturing the Avatar.

ZHAO

Ambitious and ruthless, this Fire Navy admiral will do whatever it takes to secure his personal legacy. Zhao thinks the prince is weak, but he recognizes the fire that drives Zuko and intends to make the most of it for his own personal gain.

APPA

He's a big, fluffy white sky bison with six legs and a flat paddle of a tail. He's also an Airbender in his own right—he can manipulate the wind and air currents as easily as Aang. Appa is Aang's lifelong companion.

Who Said It?

Match the character to the quote.

Iroh

Aang

Zhao

King Bumi

Sokka

Katara

Zuko

Master Pakku

Princess Yue

1. "Love each other. Respect all life. Don't run with your spears."

2. "The world needs you now. You give people hope."

3. "You must master the four elements and confront the Fire Lord. And when you do, I hope you will think like a mad genius."

4. "I don't need luck. I don't want it. I've always had to struggle and fight, and that's made me strong. . . . It's made me who I am."

5. "I'm just saying that if I had weird powers, I'd keep my 'weirdness' to myself."

6. "I see he taught you how to duck and run like a coward. But I doubt he showed you what a Firebender is truly capable of. . . ."

7. "At my age, there's really only one big surprise left, and I'd just as soon leave it a mystery."

8. "The legends say the moon was the first Waterbender. Our ancestors saw how it pushed and pulled the tides, and learned how to do it themselves."

9. "You have proven that with fierce determination, passion, and hard work, you can accomplish anything. Raw talent alone is not enough."

QUIZ

How well do you remember *Season One*?
Flex those memory muscles with this quick quiz!

1. What happened to the other Air Nomads?

A: The Fire Nation wiped them out in an attempt to break the Avatar Cycle.

2. How did the war first start?

A: Fire Lord Sozin attacked the other nations during the passing of a comet, when Firebender power was at its peak.

3. What will Aang do now that he's the Avatar?

A: He has to restore balance between the Four Nations. To do so, he must master all four bending disciplines.

4. How did Aang escape the Fire Nation when they attacked the Air Nomads?

A: He ran away and got caught in a storm. Then his Avatar powers took over and preserved him in a giant iceberg.

5. What happens when a Firebender loses control of Fire?

A: Fire destroys everything around it.

6. What is so important about Sozin's Comet?

A: A Firebender's power increases with the passing of a comet. If Aang can't master all the elements before this comet passes, Fire Lord Ozai will become too strong to beat.

7. Why did the Water Tribe split to form the Northern and Southern Tribes?

A: Some people thought the northern ice city had too many rules and limits. They broke off and formed the Southern Tribe.

8. Who saved the moon during the Siege of the North?

A: Princess Yue.

EPISODES

Use a piece of paper and a pencil to tally your correct answers. Be sure to note the category so you can complete your score.

🌀 =AIR
🌊 =WATER
🔥 =FIRE
⬜ =EARTH
⬜ =AVATAR
⭕ =NO ELEMENT
⚫ =SPIRIT WORLD

BACKGROUND:

IT'S BEEN MORE THAN ONE HUNDRED YEARS SINCE THE FIRE NATION HAS LAUNCHED ITS ATTACK AGAINST THE OTHER NATIONS. THE AVATAR HAS BEEN MISSING THE WHOLE TIME. SOME PEOPLE BELIEVE THAT THE AVATAR DISAPPEARED WHEN THE AIR NOMADS WERE WIPED OUT.

CHAPTER 1—THE BOY IN THE ICEBERG

Katara and Sokka discover a strange, tattooed boy named Aang preserved in a giant iceberg. It turns out Aang is the new Avatar, and he accidentally alerts the world to his presence when he sets off an old Fire Navy booby trap.

🌊 How do Katara and Sokka find Aang?

A: Katara quarrels with Sokka and accidentally breaks open the iceberg that holds Aang.

🌀 What does Sokka call Appa?

A: A "fluffy snot-monster."

🌀 How do Sokka and Katara first realize that Aang is an Airbender?

A: Aang sneezes and flies ten feet into the air.

Is Sokka a Waterbender?

A: No, he isn't a bender. He's a practical guy who thinks bending is pretty much a waste of time. But he's about to learn otherwise. . . .

CHAPTER 2—THE AVATAR RETURNS

Zuko takes Aang prisoner and is shocked to discover that the Avatar is just a kid. Sokka and Katara fly Appa to Zuko's Fire Navy vessel to rescue Aang, and decide to accompany Aang on his quest to find a Waterbending master.

Why is everyone surprised to discover that a twelve–year–old boy is the Avatar?

A: They were expecting the Avatar to be an old man because the last Airbender was born more than one hundred years ago.

Zuko's father is the current Fire Lord. What is his name? And what is the name of the Fire Lord that started the war against the other nations?

A: Ozai is the current Fire Lord. Fire Lord Sozin started the war.

A BIT ABOUT BENDING

Benders use their chi— their energy—to manipulate one of the four elements: Water, Earth, Fire, or Air. A bender's chi runs from his or her arms and feet, extensions of the person's body. That means a bender must use his or her arms and legs in order to bend.

What command do you give to Appa to make him fly?
1. Hup–hup
2. Yee–ha
3. Wa–hoo
4. Yip–yip

A: 4. Yip-yip.

What Waterbending attack does Katara accidentally use to rescue Aang?

A: She freezes the soldiers where they stand.

CHAPTER 3—THE SOUTHERN AIR TEMPLE

Aang leads Katara and Sokka to the Southern Air Temple hoping to find surviving Airbenders. Instead, Aang discovers the fate of his beloved father figure, Monk Gyatso, and finds statues that represent his former lives, the previous Avatars.

What is the name of the Southern Air Temple?

A: Jongmu Air Temple.

According to Aang, there is only one way to get to an Air Nomad temple. What is it?

A: On a flying bison.

Inside the temple, Aang learns that someone will guide him on his mission to master all the bending arts. Who is it?

A: The spirit of Avatar Roku.

AANG'S AMAZING STAFF

Aang uses his staff to defend against attacks in hand—to—hand combat, but it also opens up into a glider. How does Aang use this glider?

1. Magic
2. The wings help Aang harness the wind and air currents.
3. It comes with a lightweight motor.

A: 2. The wings help Aang harness the wind and air currents.

What is so important about Avatar Roku?

A: The Avatar before Aang, Roku was a powerful Firebender who opposed Fire Lord Sozin's desire to conquer the other nations. He alone kept the Fire Lord in check while he was alive. His advice is crucial.

CHAPTER 4—KYOSHI ISLAND

While Aang receives a little too much love from adoring fans on Kyoshi Island, Sokka must deal with his feelings of inadequacy when the local band of warriors— all girls—beat him in battle.

The villagers find out that Aang is the Avatar when . . .

A: He tells them he knows Avatar Kyoshi, as Avatar, he was her in a former life.

How does Aang save Kyoshi Island after the Firebender attack?

A: He uses his Airbending skills to force the giant Unagi Eel to put out the fires with its water spray.

CHAPTER 5—THE KING AND AANG

Brought before the aging king of Omashu, Aang is forced to perform a series of bizarre challenges in order to free Sokka and Katara from prison. It's as if the king knows that Aang is the Avatar. But how?

How do Aang, Sokka, and Katara get in trouble with the Omashu authorities?

A: They ride down the city's vast network of chutes like bobsledders.

What Airbending trick does Aang use to complete the king's first challenge?

A: He uses air currents to send a rock stalactite flying to retrieve a missing key. Then he uses air currents to bring it back to him.

What is the king's name and how does he know who Aang really is?

A: King Bumi is an old friend of Aang's.

CHAPTER 6—IMPRISONED

The friends arrive at an Earth Kingdom village that is occupied by the Fire Nation. The town's Earthbenders have been imprisoned and are so demoralized that they are unable to fight back. Katara decides to start an Earthbender revolt.

○ What's the name of the young Earthbender that Katara befriends?

A: Haru.

What is the Earthbender prison made of?

A: Metal. (Most Earthbenders can't bend metal!)

Sokka realizes there is something in the prison that the Earthbenders can bend. What is it?

A: Coal.

CHAPTER 7—WINTER SOLSTICE, PART 1: THE SPIRIT WORLD

Aang must quickly learn how to get to the Spirit World in order to save Sokka, who's been captured by an angry forest spirit. Once there, Aang meets a dragon spirit who gives him a mission: Make contact with Avatar Roku.

Why do people think Aang knows how to enter the Spirit World?

A: The Avatar is the bridge between the Mortal World and the Spirit World.

What is the name of the angry forest spirit?

A: Hei Bai.

What shape does the forest spirit take when Aang appeases it?

A: A panda.

Why does a dragon spirit appear?

A: This is the spirit of Avatar Roku's animal guide and he has a message for Aang from Roku.

What important discovery does Aang make about the limitations of the Spirit World?

A: You can't bend in the Spirit World!

CHAPTER 8—WINTER SOLSTICE, PART 2: AVATAR ROKU

Aang has to get to Crescent Island to make contact with the spirit of Avatar Roku. He makes it with minutes to spare, but he faces danger when he emerges: Commander Zhao, along with Zuko and Iroh, are waiting to ambush him.

Where is Crescent Island?

A: In the heart of Fire Nation territory!

Where does Aang have to go to make contact with the spirit of Roku?

A: A temple that holds a statue of Avatar Roku, guarded by Fire Sages who are loyal to the Fire Lord.

What is the name of the Fire Sage who is loyal to the Avatar?

A: Shyu.

Which spirit helps Aang get past Zhao and the other Firebenders?

A: The spirit of Avatar Roku takes over Aang's body—only another powerful Firebender could defeat Zhao and his men.

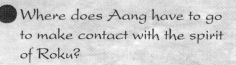

CHAPTER 9—THE WATERBENDING SCROLL

Katara "borrows" a Waterbending scroll so she and Aang can learn more Waterbending moves. Unfortunately, the scroll belongs to pirates who recruit Zuko to help recover the scroll.

Why does Katara get mad when she and Aang study the scroll together?

A: Aang picks up the Waterbending moves faster than she does!

What simple yet powerful move do Katara and Aang master with the help of the scroll?

A: The single water whip.

What handy device does Aang grab when Katara picks up the scroll?

A: A special bison whistle that only Appa can hear.

CHAPTER 10—JET

Katara, Sokka, and Aang are saved from an ambush by a band of young Earth Kingdom rebels. These self-styled freedom fighters are led by Jet, a charismatic teen who tries to enlist the Avatar's help in the fight against the Fire Nation.

While walking through the woods, Katara suggests that Aang lead the way because he is the Avatar. Why does Sokka disagree?

A: Sokka says Aang is just a goofy kid. (And Aang agrees!)

What special mission does Jet have for Aang and Katara?

A: He tells them he needs their help filling the reservoir with water to save the forest from being burned. (Instead, he plans to use them to flood out the entire valley.)

JET

Orphaned at a young age by Firebenders, Jet vows to make as much trouble as he can for the Fire Nation. To that end, he and his band of followers—others orphaned by Fire Nation soldiers—disrupt supply lines, mount ambushes, and more.

○ Can you name the members of Jet's band of freedom fighters?

A: Sneers, Longshot, Pipsqueak, the Duke, and Smellerbee.

CHAPTER 11—THE GREAT DIVIDE

Is settling feuds and making peace all in a day's work for the Avatar? Aang finds out the hard way when he must mediate between two long-feuding tribes of refugees during a trek through the Great Divide.

○ What are the names of the two tribes?

A: Zhangs and Gan Jins.

What advice does Aang give the refugees when they fight one another?

A: "Harsh words won't solve problems. Actions will."

Aang says he knows Wei Jin and Jin Wei, the two men in the story at the heart of the tribes' conflict. How does Aang know them?

A: He doesn't. Aang makes up this small fib for the sake of peace between the tribes.

CHAPTER 12—THE STORM

When he is confronted by a fisherman, Aang learns that not everyone thinks the reappearance of the Avatar is good news. Aang runs off, consumed with guilt about his one-hundred-year-long absence. Meanwhile, Zuko is having his own command problems, and Iroh explains Zuko's history to the crew.

Why did Aang run away from the Southern Air Temple one hundred years ago?

1. He refused to be separated from Monk Gyatso.
2. He didn't think he was smart enough.
3. He wanted to play professional sky bison polo.

A: 1. He refused to be separated from Monk Gyatso.

How old are Airbender Avatars when they are informed of their true abilities?

A: They are sixteen. But Aang was told earlier because the monks felt the new Avatar was needed right away.

THE GREAT DIVIDE

How did the Great Divide form?

A: Experts say it was carved into the Earth by spirits who were angry with local farmers for not offering them a proper sacrifice.

CHAPTER 13—THE BLUE SPIRIT

Aang gets ambushed by the Fire Nation and learns that Zhao plans to lock him up for the rest of his life—kept just barely alive—so that the Avatar can never reincarnate! Enter the mysterious Blue Spirit, who frees Aang in the nick of time.

⬤ Is the Blue Spirit a real spirit?

A: No—it's Zuko in disguise!

◯ What special weapon does the Blue Spirit use to rescue Aang?

A: Twin broadswords.

◯ What remedy does Aang give to Katara and Sokka to make them better?

A: He gives them frozen wood-frogs to suck on.

CHAPTER 14—THE FORTUNE-TELLER

Do fortunes, once told, always come true? Aang and Sokka discover that a village of believers lies in the path of an active volcano that is about to erupt—despite the fortune-teller's prediction to the contrary.

〰 What good news does Katara get from the fortune-teller, Aunt Wu?

A: That she is destined to marry a great bender.

How do Aang and Sokka convince the villagers that the volcano is dangerous?

1. They manipulate the clouds to get Aunt Wu to change her prediction.
2. They say Aunt Wu lied.
3. They say the stars predict the volcano will blow.

A: 1. They manipulate the clouds to get Aunt Wu to change her prediction.

What advice does the fortune-teller give Aang?

A: That he can shape his own destiny.

CHAPTER 15—BATO OF THE WATER TRIBE

Sokka and Katara run into an old friend from home and suddenly Aang feels left out. After a misunderstanding, Aang decides to head off on his own. Meanwhile, Zuko hires a bounty hunter to track the Avatar with help from a beast called the Shirshu.

What important information does Aang keep from Sokka and Katara?

A: A map that shows where they can meet Hakoda, their father.

What Water Tribe rite of passage did Sokka miss out on when the men of his tribe left for war?

A: Ice dodging.

21

How does Aang assist Sokka in this rite of passage?

A: He controls the jib. He also uses a bit of Airbending.

Match the charcter to the mark
Bato gives him/her:

Sokka   Trusted

Katara   Wise

Aang   Brave

BRAVE

WISE

TRUSTED

A: Sokka (wise), Katara (brave), Aang (trusted)

CHAPTER 16—THE DESERTER

A Firebending master, Jeong Jeong, agrees to teach Aang. Aang is so excited that he lets his fire get out of control and accidentally burns Katara. Katara heals quickly, but Aang is devastated, and he vows never to Firebend again.

According to Jeong Jeong, what will fire do if one can't control it?

A: It will destroy everything in its path.

Name one of Jeong Jeong's former students.

A: Zhao.

What secret does Katara learn about herself when Aang burns her?

A: She learns that she, like other powerful Waterbenders, has healing powers.

CHAPTER 17—THE GLIDERS

Might there be some surviving Airbenders after all? Aang, Katara, and Sokka discover a group of refugees in the ruins of the Northern Air Temple. They are led by a brilliant inventor, the Mechanist, who is paying the Fire Nation for freedom by giving them high-tech weaponry.

How does Aang know from far away that the people flying around the temple are not Airbenders?

A: He can tell they lack "spirit" by the way they move.

What does Aang think of the Mechanist's improvements to the temple?

A: He thinks the whole place stinks! Parts of the old temple—sacred to his people—were destroyed to make way for new technology.

The Mechanist creates a special machine to help his wheelchair-bound son. What Airbender tool inspired him?

A: Airbender gliders inspired him to build light flying machines.

The Mechanist decides to stop giving technology to the Fire Nation army, but not before they manage to take possession of a very important weapon. What is it?

A: A war balloon that can be used to drop bombs.

CHAPTER 18—THE WATERBENDING MASTER

Having finally reached the Northern Water Tribe and locating a Waterbending master, the friends are outraged to discover that it's against the rules for girls to Waterbend. Katara also discovers a family secret about her beloved grandmother.

What are Waterbender girls allowed to do in the Northern Water Tribe?

A: They are permitted to develop their healing powers.

What truth does Katara learn about her grandmother?

A: She discovers that Gran Gran fled to the Southern Water Tribe to escape an arranged marriage to the waterbending master, Pakku.

How does Katara convince Master Pakku to teach her after all?

A: She challenges him to fight her . . . and very nearly wins!

CHAPTER 19—THE SIEGE OF THE NORTH, PART 1

Admiral Zhao means to capture the Avatar but Zuko hopes to get to the Avatar first. Meanwhile, Aang seeks help from the Spirit World to fight the Fire Nation navy. He enters the Spirit World minutes before Zuko arrives to drag Aang's body off into the frozen wilderness.

🌀 While Aang and Katara are busy Waterbending, who occupies Sokka's time?

A: The chief's daughter, Princess Yue.

🌀 Sokka and Princess Yue become fast friends. More than friends, in fact. But what keeps this couple apart?

A: Like many other girls of the Northern Water Tribe, Yue wears a betrothal necklace. Her husband has already been chosen for her.

🌀 Why does the princess have white hair?

A: When Yue was a baby, she was quite sickly. But when the Moon Spirit touched the baby and gave her some of its life energy, she was cured. The experience turned Yue's hair white.

🌀 Where does Aang meditate in order to enter the Spirit World?

A: The Spirit Oasis.

CHAPTER 20—THE SIEGE OF THE NORTH, PART 2

Back in the mortal world, Katara and Sokka rescue Aang's body. All return to the city in time to see Zhao kidnap the moon in mortal form. This has been Zhao's plan all along—to break the Water Tribe's power by destroying its source: the moon itself.

🌀 What happens to Aang's spirit when it returns to the Spirit Oasis?

A: It nearly doesn't find its way back to Aang's body! Luckily, Aang's body sucks his spirit back into place.

What is another way to describe the Moon and Ocean spirits?

1. Tui and La
2. Push and Pull
3. Yin and Yang
4. All of the above

A: 4. All of the above.

What other mortal besides Aang can see spirits while they are in the Spirit World?

A: Iroh. He sees Aang ride the spirit dragon, and he can see that Yue has been touched by the Moon Spirit.

When talking to Koh, why can't Aang show emotion?

A: Koh will steal his face if he does.

How did Koh anger one of Aang's earlier incarnations?

A: Koh stole the face of the Avatar's beloved.

BONUS QUIZ:
NAME THAT CREATURE!

The Avatar world is filled with all sorts of interesting creatures! You're already familiar with sky bison and flying lemurs. How many others can you identify?

UNAGI EEL • TURTLE-DUCKS • KOMODO-RHINOS
MONGOOSE-DRAGONS • SABER-TOOTHED MOOSE-LIONS
CANYON CRAWLERS • BUZZARD-WASPS • PENGUINS • SHIRSHU

1. One of these cute and cuddly little fellas was nicknamed "Mr. FooFoo Cuddly Poofs" by Sokka.

2. Strong, sturdy, and with extra—tough hides, these are often used by Fire Nation soldiers.

3. Aang just loves sledding with these guys!

4. Azula, Ty Lee, and Mai ride these amazing creatures. They can run across water!

5. One of these water birds attacked a young Prince Zuko.

6. Appa finds a nest of these when he's separated from Aang.

7. This monstrous creature tracks by scent. It also has venom—laced spit that can paralyze a full—grown man.

8. Don't eat food near these gigantic critters. The smell alone draws them out of their cave hiding places.

ANSWERS: 1. saber-toothed moose-lions 2. Komodo-rhinos 3. penguins 4. mongoose-dragons 5. turtle-ducks 6. buzzard-wasps 7. Shirshu 8. Canyon Crawlers

Season Two
BOOK TWO: EARTH

CAST OF CHARACTERS

You've finished with Book One: Water. Now it's time to consider Book Two: Earth. Who are the main characters? Who did what? Here's another quick refresher course.

IROH

Zuko's uncle is a powerful Firebender and a legendary warrior. But he also has an acute sense of the four elements and the importance of balance. He loves his nephew very much and keeps a close eye on him.

TOPH

This petite daughter of one of the Earth Kingdom's wealthiest families may be blind, but she certainly isn't helpless. Toph's blindness has actually helped her to "see" better with her other senses. She calls herself the world's most powerful Earthbender. And she is!

AZULA

Zuko's younger sister is a Firebending prodigy. She has mastered the "cold-blooded fire"—lightning. She is precise and calculating, and she plans to beat her brother to the prize: the Avatar.

TY LEE

Acrobatic Ty Lee is an old school pal of Azula's. She's flexible, fast on her feet, and has mastered a series of chi-blocking punches that can disable the careless bender who allows her to get too close.

LONG FENG

This Earthbender is proof that you don't need to be a king to have complete power. As the Earth King's cultural minister, Long Feng has built his own shadow government, backed by the secret police known as the Dai Li.

MAI

Another of Azula's school friends, Mai is a fearsome Firebender in her own right. Easily bored and always restless, she is the perfect complement to Azula. She understands what needs doing without much explanation, and she doesn't let emotions get in her way.

Whodunnit?

Match the character with the quote.

Azula • Ty Lee • General Fong
Professor Zei • Huu • the Earth King
Mai • Long Feng • Toph • Lee

1. The Avatar is our ultimate weapon! With him leading the way, we can cut right through the Fire Nation. He just needs to get in touch with his "inner Avatar." And I'm just the man to help.

2. I received total enlightenment and now I live to protect the swamp from any human who tries to hurt it. I can even bend the water inside of plants to make myself special jungle armor!

3. My father wanted me to make a deal: exchange a king for the life of my brother. But my friend said she didn't think it was a fair exchange. You know, she's right. So I walked out on my brother.

4. I just saw the cutest boy! I kept trying to get close to him, but he kept backing away. It's like we were dancing or something! Oh, well. I'm sure there will be a next time!

5. I've had no luck using the regular channels to handle the Avatar. Perhaps a missing animal would help convince him to back off.

6. That Twinkle Toes sure is tricky. I can't do anything to get him to stand up to me. Hmmm. Maybe if I steal some of his nuts and then use his precious stick to crack them, then I'll get a rise out of him.

7. I sure owe that stranger! When I egged that thug, he and his gang blamed the stranger and they took his feed. Well, I'll take him home and feed his mount. That's the least I can do to thank him for not ratting me out.

8. With help from my maps, the Avatar and his friends were able to find the long-lost library of Wan Shi Tong, the undiscovered jewel of the desert! But the Great Knowledge Spirit got angry and buried the library. I couldn't bear to part with those precious books, so I refused to leave.

9. I just found the perfect way to infiltrate Ba Sing Se! Those Kyoshi warriors have no need of their armor now. Instead, we'll be the Earth King's loyal servants. . . .

10. These children keep insisting that there's a secret war going on, but how could that be? My trusted advisor has told me nothing of any war! It sounds like a crazy conspiracy theory to me, but I suppose the matter is worth looking into. Perhaps if the bald one gives me a ride on his sky bison . . .

ANSWERS: 1. General Fong 2. Huu 3. Mai 4. Ty Lee 5. Long Feng 6. Toph 7. Lee 8. Professor Zci 9. Azula 10. the Earth King

31

EPISODES

Use a piece of paper and a pencil to continue tallying your correct answers. Be sure to note the category so you can complete your score.

= AIR

= WATER

= FIRE

= EARTH

= AVATAR

= NO ELEMENT

= SPIRIT WORLD

CHAPTER 1—THE AVATAR STATE

An Earth Kingdom general is convinced that victory against the Fire Lord will soon be achieved. He just needs one more thing: Aang in the Avatar state. The problem is that Aang can't control it, he doesn't know how to trigger it, and quite frankly, he's scared of the power.

When they leave for the Earth Kingdom, Master Pakku gives Katara and Aang gifts. What does he give Sokka?
1. A new boomerang
2. A pat on the shoulder
3. A stash of blubber—seal jerky

A: 2. A pat on the shoulder.

What methods does General Fong use to trigger the Avatar state in Aang?
1. Chi—enhancing tea
2. The symbolic joining of the four elements
3. Endangering Aang's life
4. All of the above

A: 4. All of the above.

🔷 What finally does trigger Aang's Avatar state?

A: A threat to Katara's life.

🔶 Whom does the Fire Lord send to clean up Zuko's "mess" from season one?

A: Zuko's younger sister, Azula.

STATE SECRETS

The spirit of Avatar Roku explains the true nature of the Avatar state to Aang. It's really a super defense mechanism designed to give the current Avatar access to the skills and knowledge of all the past Avatars.

🔷 What is the secret vulnerability of the Avatar state?

A: All the past Avatar spirits are contained in one being. If the Avatar is killed while in this state, that's the end of the Avatar Cycle. So an Avatar's greatest power is also his most profound weakness.

CHAPTER 2—THE CAVE OF TWO LOVERS

The only way past the Fire Nation to Omashu is a secret love cave—a labyrinth created by two lovers inside a mountain. The key to safe passage, the story goes, is to trust in the power of love. Otherwise, Aang, Katara, and Sokka could be trapped forever.

How do Aang and Katara find their way out of the labyrinth?

A: When their torch dies out, they discover a secret path made of luminescent crystals.

What creatures help Zuko find his way out?

A: Giant badger-moles.

Where do Zuko and Iroh decide to go after events at the North Pole?
1. Home, to the Fire Nation and prison
2. To the Earth Kingdom, to hide as refugees
3. They plan to join the Avatar

A: 2. To the Earth Kingdom, to hide as refugees.

THE FIRST EARTHBENDERS

While in the tunnel system, Aang and Katara learn about the first Earthbenders, the two lovers in the story. Meeting secretly to hide their love, they watched the badger-moles dig through the mountain and taught themselves to Earthbend.

What were the names of these lovers?

A: The woman was called Oma, and the man was named Shu. The city Omashu was named to remember their great love.

CHAPTER 3—RETURN TO OMASHU

The Fire Nation has taken over Omashu! Worse, King Bumi is nowhere to be found. Aang is determined to rescue his old friend, while Sokka and Katara are equally determined to help Omashu's refugees fake a deadly plague—pentapox—so they can escape the city.

Why does Aang need King Bumi?

A: He wants Bumi to teach him Earthbending.

Why did Bumi surrender to his captors?

A: As he tells Aang, he's waiting for the right moment, and then he'll take back his city.

What is Azula doing in Omashu?

A: She wants to recruit her old friend, Mai—the daughter of Omashu's new governor—for her special fighting force.

CHAPTER 4—THE SWAMP

Aang leads his friends into the heart of a swamp. There they meet up with a hermit who explains that the swamp is really one giant living organism that has spread out its roots over a vast area. As Avatar, Aang can learn how to listen to this organism.

Aang sees a vision of the future while in the swamp. What does he see?

A: A laughing girl in a pretty dress—his future Earthbending master.

Appa and Momo get lost in the jungle. How does Aang find them?

A: He listens to the earth and the living swamp tells him where to find them.

🌀 Who is the Swamp Monster?

A: Huu, a hermit who has learned to bend water inside swamp vegetation to make himself a giant plantlike suit of armor. He uses his disguise to protect the swamp.

🌀 Who else do Katara and Sokka meet in the swamp?

A: Other Waterbenders who must be distant kin.

CHAPTER 5—AVATAR DAY

Aang allows himself to be put on trial in a small village in order to clear the name of Avatar Kyoshi. Meanwhile, Katara and Sokka go back to Kyoshi Island to uncover the truth. But is truth and justice even possible when the villagers refuse to consider the evidence?

THE BIRTH OF KYOSHI ISLAND

The spirit of Avatar Kyoshi explains that Chin was a greedy tyrant who wanted nothing more than to build his empire at the expense of others. The Avatar tried to negotiate with him, but he refused all peaceful solutions.

On Avatar Day, the villagers . . .

A: Burn a statue and yell, "Down with the Avatar!"

Why is Aang on trial?

A: The villagers hold Avatar Kyoshi responsible for the loss of their ancient leader, Chin.

What happened when Chin tried to take over the Avatar's village?

A: Avatar Kyoshi used her great power to separate the village from the mainland and protect her people. The village became Kyoshi Island.

What happened to Chin?

A: When Avatar Kyoshi separated her village from the mainland, the ground beneath Chin's feet gave way and he fell, never to return.

CHAPTER 6—THE BLIND BANDIT

Could a twelve-year-old blind girl be the Earthbending master Aang is looking for? Aang sure thinks so. Recognizing the girl of his vision, Aang watches Toph closely. Despite her handicap, she knocks everyone else flat. But her parents know nothing of her skills.

What advice did Bumi give Aang about finding an Earthbending master?

A: To look for a teacher who "listens to the earth."

Who is the Blind Bandit?

A: Toph, the blind daughter of a wealthy businessman, keeps her considerable skills secret from her parents. But she has a secret identity for Earthbending tournaments: the Blind Bandit.

What's Toph's nickname for Aang?

A: Twinkle Toes.

CHAPTER 7—ZUKO ALONE

Traveling through the countryside on his own, Zuko meets a small boy, Lee, and his family. When the boy gets in trouble with some local thugs, will Zuko stand by and let it happen, or will he save Lee with his Firebending and reveal his identity?

◯ Lee makes friends with Zuko because . . .

A: Lee egged the thugs and Zuko took the blame.

🔥 What happened to Lee's older brother?

A: He was taken prisoner and forced to join the Fire Nation army.

🔥 Zuko gives Lee a knife with an inscription on the blade. What is the inscription?

A: "Never give up without a fight."

CHAPTER 8—THE CHASE

Someone in a scary-looking tank is tracking Aang and his friends, and nothing seems able to stop it! The attackers: Princess Azula and her special fighting force made up of two school friends, Ty Lee and Mai.

How does Azula continue to track Aang, even when he's flying?

A: Appa is shedding his winter fur and is leaving an easy trail to follow.

🔥 What skill makes Ty Lee especially dangerous?

A: She has special chi-blocking punches that can disable benders!

Separated at one point from Aang and the others, Toph strikes up a new friendship with whom?

A: Iroh.

CHAPTER 9—BITTER WORK

Earthbending turns out to be much harder than Aang expects. Toph tells him he must root himself to the ground like a rock. It sounds simple, but it goes against Aang's light and breezy Airbender nature.

Reunited with his uncle, Zuko starts training again. Iroh shares what surprising Firebending secret?

A: Some of Iroh's moves come from watching benders of the other elements.

Why can't Zuko create lightning?

A: Lightning is a pure expression of Firebending, without emotion. Zuko has too much emotion inside him to create lightning.

Who (besides Iroh) is able to produce lightning while Firebending?

A: Azula.

CHAPTER 10—THE LIBRARY

Looking for Fire Nation weaknesses, Sokka urges the group to find an ancient library. But its guardian spirit doesn't trust humans. Can Sokka dig out some Fire Nation secrets? He's got minutes before the protective spirit buries the library altogether.

 What is the name of the spirit that guards the library, and what form does it take?

A: Wan Shi Tong takes the form of an owl.

Who helps the group find the library?

A: Professor Zei.

As Toph struggles to keep the library from sinking, what happens?

A: Mysterious Sandbenders capture Appa and spirit him away, right under her nose!

THE LIBRARY OF WAN SHI TONG

According to legend, the Great Knowledge Spirit, Wan Shi Tong, collected a vast library. With the help of his fox-shaped assistants, he amassed books and scrolls from all over the world so mankind could read them and become better people. But experience taught Wan Shi Tong that people will try to use his knowledge to get an edge on other people.

What information did Zhao learn in Wan Shi Tong's library?

A: The mortal identities of the Moon and Ocean Spirits.

CHAPTER 11—THE DESERT

Aang scours the desert for Appa while Katara does her best to lead the others through the sun and sand to the Earth King in Ba Sing Se. They need his backing to plan an attack on the Fire Lord.

What important Fire Nation secret does Sokka want to share with the Earth King?

A: They must attack the Fire Nation during the next solar eclipse, when Firebenders are powerless.

Now refugees in the Earth Kingdom capital, Zuko and Iroh find help from what secret society?

A: The Order of the White Lotus.

Why does Katara lead? Isn't Toph, as an Earthbender, a better choice for a guide?

A: Toph can't "see" in the desert—the sand isn't solid enough for her to use her Earthbending abilities.

WATER POWER

A Waterbender's power is dependent on the presence of water, so many Waterbenders carry a skin of water for emergencies.

What happens when Momo spills their precious water in the desert?

A: Katara is so skilled that she can bend the spilled water back into the skin before it is lost.

CHAPTER 12—THE SERPENT'S PASS

Traveling sure is tougher when you can't fly! Aang and his friends help a needy family get to Ba Sing Se via the dangerous route—the dreaded Serpent's Pass. Luckily, they receive some unexpected help from an old friend.

◯ Who is the old friend that helps Aang, Katara, and Sokka guide the family through the pass?

A: Suki, the Kyoshi warrior.

◯ When Zuko and Iroh take the easy way to Ba Sing Se—the ferry—whom do they meet?

A: Jet and some of his gang.

◯ What surprising piece of information does Iroh learn about Smellerbee?

A: Smellerbee is a girl!

◉ What does Toph use at border control to get tickets for the ferry to Ba Sing Se?

A: The Golden Seal of the Flying Boar.

CHAPTER 13—THE DRILL

Approaching Ba Sing Se by monorail, Aang, Katara, Toph, and Sokka spy a huge mechanical drill being used by the Fire Nation to break through the walls of the city. Do the friends have what it takes to disable the drill?

The Earth Kingdom generals think the drill is . . .

A: Not a real threat. They believe the city walls will hold.

What slip of Firebending nearly gives away Iroh and Zuko?

A: Jet figures out that Iroh must have used Firebending to heat up a cup of cold tea.

How does Aang break his busboy disguise at the Oval Palace?

A: He spills water on a lady and Airbends her dry.

Which Firebender once got close to breaching the walls of Ba Sing Se?

A: The Dragon of the West—Iroh!

CHAPTER 14—CITY OF WALLS AND SECRETS

Inside the walls of Ba Sing Se at last, all that's left is to tell the Earth King of the danger. Simple, right? But mazes of strict rules keep everyone—the Avatar included—away from the Earth King.

How long will the friends have to wait to see the Earth King?

A: About a month.

The Earth King's pet, Bosco, is a very rare species in the Avatar world. What kind of animal is he?
1. An opossum
2. A bear
3. A dog
4. A parrot

A: 2. A bear.

CHAPTER 15—THE TALES OF BA SING SE

In this series of brief stories, each about a different important character, the personal adventures of Katara, Toph, Iroh, Sokka, Aang, Zuko, and even Momo are explored in greater detail.

⬭ A robber nearly mugs Iroh. What happens instead?

A: Iroh makes friends with the man and gives him tips on his fighting stance.

🔥 What is the name of Iroh's son?

A: Lu Ten.

⬭ In Sokka's tale, Sokka competes in a poetry competition with the teacher of a group of elegant young ladies. What is the name of the group?

A: The group is called the Five Seven Five Society for the number of syllables allowed in each poem (haiku).

🌀 Momo finds a clue to Appa's whereabouts, but he doesn't notice it. What is the clue?

A: Appa's gigantic paw print.

CHAPTER 16—APPA'S LOST DAYS

How has Appa been faring during his separation from Aang? This episode takes viewers back to the sinking of Wan Shi Tong's library in order to learn how Appa was captured, where he's been, and who he's met along the way.

🪨 What do the Sandbenders want with Appa?

A: They want as much money as possible; they plan to sell him to the highest bidder.

Where does Appa go when he doesn't know where to find Aang?

A: He heads for home—the Eastern Air Temple where he was born.

CHAPTER 17—LAKE LAOGAI

The friends continue their search for Appa with posters and leaflets. Who turns up, wanting to help? Jet! What no one—not even Jet himself—realizes is that Jet is a Dai Li spy. Are the Dai Li holding Appa? Will the friends find him? Not if a certain Firebending prince has anything to say about it. . . .

Where are the Dai Li keeping Appa?

A: In a secret headquarters beneath Lake Laogai.

What is the trigger phrase that the Dai Li use to brainwash their victims?

A: "The Earth King has invited you to Lake Laogai."

Who frees Appa?

A: Zuko.

CHAPTER 18—THE EARTH KING

Aang and his friends now have a dual mission: to enlist the Earth King's support in the fight against the Fire Lord and expose Long Feng. But the clueless Earth King isn't even aware that there is a war going on because Long Feng has kept it a secret!

How does Long Feng try to explain away the presence of the Fire Nation drill if there is no war?

A: He says it is is a construction project. . . that just happens to have a Fire Nation emblem on its side!

Zuko falls ill with a fever. What causes it?

A: Zuko's good deed—freeing Appa—causes a spiritual crisis that threatens to harm him.

Who are the Red and Blue Dragons of Zuko's fever dream?

A: The Blue Dragon speaks with Azula's voice. The Red Dragon speaks with Iroh's voice. They represent the two halves of Zuko's spirit.

CHAPTER 19—THE GURU

Aang begins training with a guru who promises to teach him to control the Avatar state. Meanwhile, Toph is captured by bounty hunters, and Katara finds Firebenders in Ba Sing Se. She tells the Kyoshi warriors, but the Kyoshi warriors are not who they seem.

Who are the Kyoshi warriors that come to serve the Earth King?

A: They are Azula, Mai, and Ty Lee in disguise.

Why are bounty hunters after Toph?

A: Toph's parents sent them—they think that she's been taken by the Avatar.

What vital secret does the Earth King give away to Azula when he thinks that she's a Kyoshi warrior?

A: He tells her that his army plans to invade the Fire Nation on the Day of the Black Sun—the solar eclipse.

GURU PATHIK

This old friend of Monk Gyatso helps Aang gain control of the Avatar state by teaching Aang to clear out his chakras—spiraling pools of energy in his body. Doing this will allow Aang to find balance within himself so he can bring balance to the rest of the world.

🀄 What special drink does Guru Pathik give Aang during this process?

A: Onion and banana juice.

CHAPTER 20—THE CROSSROADS OF DESTINY

Both Aang and Zuko face their destinies and make final choices. Aang realizes that he might have sacrificed the many to save the one (Katara). Is it too late to choose again? Should Zuko join his sister and reclaim his inheritance, or will he choose good, as his uncle urges? The fate of the world hangs in the balance.

🀄 What friend of Toph shows up to help the Avatar when he needs it most?

A: Iroh.

🀄 Katara uses the water from the Spirit Oasis to . . .

A: Heal Aang after he is harmed while in the Avatar state.

🔥 Why is Iroh called "The Dragon of the West"?

A: Because he can Firebend using his own breath, just like a dragon.

YOUR SCORE, REVEALED!

Give yourself a point for every correct response to the episode quiz questions and add up the total.

106—140 points:
You have attained total Avatar enlightenment! Your chakras are clear and you are ready to attain the Avatar state!

71—105 points:
You have a good head on your shoulders! You are a ready student of the bending arts and you are on the brink of attaining mastery!

36—70 points:
You have made a good beginning! Your determination will pay off with continued effort.

0—35 points:
Discipline is the key to success in the bending arts. Proceed with your studies and try again.

Now look at your scores for each category. Did you do better in some categories in comparison to others? Perhaps you scored well in the Earth category, but not the Air category. Air and Earth are opposites. You may be such a strong Earthbender that the Air questions simply elude you. Perhaps bending isn't for you; maybe you were born to be a scholar of the Spirit World. Or did you do equally well in all categories? You may have what it takes to be the next Avatar!